Triumphs, Trials, and Tribulations

Collection of Life's Ups and Downs

D. Renee' Clifton

India | USA | UK

Dedication

Life has a way of keeping you humble, and I have been lucky enough to have three incredible individuals who keep me firmly grounded in reality. It is because of them that I survive. Each gives me their own special reason for knowing that the world is a better place!

Mom- You are the world's greatest cheerleader! You have always breathed life into my hopes and dreams. It is your strength and support that lets me know that I can do anything I want to do. It is because you still put my school picture on the refrigerator that lets me know I can always be a kid at heart and that it will always be okay to never grow up. For all that is good in me, it is there because of you.

Sarah- The moment that you took your first breath, I knew magic was real and miracles truly exist. I saw the world outside of myself for the very first time. As you grew, so too did your spirit, and I couldn't be happier for that. You have always been my biggest critic, but you are also my best friend! You are all the "right" decisions I have ever made in my life. You are that conservative end of the spectrum of your mother, and I can't wait to place that hood on you, Dr. Fleenor.

Brad- The moment that you took your first breath was the moment that I realized I would never stop worrying about you! The fear that I wouldn't know how to be a mother to a boy fell instantly away as I gazed at your precious face. As you grew, I saw that you are all the "crazy" and "wild" decisions I have ever made in life. Ours is a special "drive each other crazy and love each other fiercely" relationship! You are that free-spirited end of the spectrum of your mother, and I cherish watching the parent that you are becoming as your own child grows. You are a wonderful daddy!

Kids, you have weathered storms that have tempered sailors far older and far more experienced than yourselves. I will forever strive to fill all the voids that those storms created. Let me know where I need to patch any holes that threaten to spring a leak. SMILE!

One last "individual" deserves recognition-. . .

Lucy- You have been the sweetest girl, the most dedicated roommate, and worst dog I have ever been lucky enough to love and live with. SMILE! You keep me straight and closely monitor my moods. Your never ceasing ability to "read me" is precious, sweet girl! Mommy loves you.

I love all of you, dearly!

Renee' (MOM)

Acknowledgement

To all of you who have taught me invaluable lessons- and you know who you are- thank you! There have been many that sent me soaring to the heights of the heavens. There have been many that brought me to my knees. I'm grateful for all of them. You can't just have the good without the bad. Through it all, family centered in love, words, and music, and friends centered in support and happiness keep life worth living!

Preface

Attempting to capture emotions from the heart and soul and turn them into words is perhaps the hardest and yet one of the most rewarding parts of my day! Life can be hellish or heavenly, but still, the words flow to the page. Oftentimes, there's some unexplained internal urgency demanding that I put pen to paper. As difficult as those moments may be, it is the most liberating experience I can offer myself.

Breathless

Breathless
I want to leave you breathless
Helpless for me
Turn your world upside down
You know not how
To recover from my touch, my whispered sound

I touch your body, your soul
We're losing control
My hands grip-hold you tight
We fight against the edge
Your pulse quickens,
Lost in the sheets
Our eyes meet
In the heat of the moment
I smile to see you breathless
While I'm left helpless.

Your gaze you can't disguise,
Your hands, your eyes,
They don't lie.
Your heated kiss falls on my lips
I reach to wipe your brow
And now I'm the helpless one,
Coming undone.

Slowly, deeply,
More sweetly we grow
The tenderest of moments play out
Our eyes betray us in a crowd,
Our worlds are turned upside down
We know not how to recover
From the touch, the feel, the sound.
Our passion leaves us
Both breathless,
Helpless for each other.

Bit-by-Bit

He smiled to himself when I said goodbye.
He was too weak to leave me on his own, so
he broke me down bit-by-bit,
It would be sad, were it not so cruel
the hell I'd been through...
but it's a new day.

He's got his quiet little world back, and
here I stand
I may have come out, for once, on top

It wasn't like I didn't love him. I gave my all.
He didn't know what that meant, so I sent
him off with my goodbye.
Even then, bit-by-bit, he still walked blindly
away.

They say, when one door closes, another
opens. . .
A new soul comes to mend a heart; take your
part—
But I'm afraid to start.

Chasing Away Monsters

The keys play a tune that once brought solace
to my soul.
A hole resides there now, carved by loss.
Despair has clouded my vision; no decision is
made with conviction.
All I desire is to run and hide
To find that little girl who still finds monsters
under her bed,
But where mother is there to soothe her fears
and
Where Daddy sings away her tears.

Eyes Wide Open

You revealed your game of deceit to me,
And I knew I had been played.
I admit, it wasn't all your fault.
I felt myself driftin' away, but you didn't care
Whether the game was honest or fair
I throw down my cards, and this game is
closin'
From now on, I'm livin' life with my eyes
wide open.

Let the rain come.
Let it pour.
I've been to hell; I am not there anymore.
Though I nearly drowned at times
I am finally above the brine
Sittin' here hopin', livin' life with my eyes
wide open

I am beaten- I am battered
Frankly, that's not what matters.
All the secrets you left in your wake
Could have left me shattered
I made my choice. I knew I could take it.

Now, I'm dealin' my own hands
I'm copin'.
I'm livin' life with my eyes wide open.

What I thought was love
Was just an illusion,
Meant to keep me blind.
But only true, true love lasts forever
Anything less can easily be severed.
I realized that in the end, when I opened my
eyes.
I lift my face to the rains,
It doesn't bother me.
I've weathered the storm.
I'm copin'.
I'm finally livin' my life with my eyes wide
open.

* Love to Daddy for helping me revise this poem back in 2022

Fairy Tales

You walk the line
Between reality
And what you wish could be.
You never learned, girl,
How to roll with destiny,
So your heart's not left behind.

Fact and fiction are two
Very different things.
You try to fool yourself—
The Princess has a fairy godmother
Who flies on gossamer wings,
And the evil witch is always doomed.
But fairytales aren't real, girl
And you always find yourself
Crying the blues
In your crazy head
Love is fair,
Prince Charming descends from frogs,
And making that glass slipper fit
Is your only care.
But piecing your broken heart back together
Is what you should do instead.

Girl, you need to start
Reading between the lines.
Fairy tales are created by fools.
There is no Prince Charming
Only Big Bad Wolves
You opened the door
You saw all the signs
Truth is. . .
You were the one creating the shards
Of your own broken heart.

Fire to Flame

once tamed,
her soul
now
set free
whole
life's not played safe
dancing barefoot
now
fire to flame
nothing's the same
now
freedom's found within
her own escape into desire.

Golden Ticket

Feelin' like a damn fool, left by the side of the
road
With nowhere left to go.
I bought the ticket you were selling, I'll give
you that.
As I walked out of the darkness; there you sat,
offering me the sun
Your words were magic to my ears, calming
my fears.
I was buying all you offered.

Soon, I realized your pitch and stopped the
spree.
Were you the weak one? Not man enough,
darling, to go the distance?
Afraid to continue the dance with me?
I may be lousy at reading the signs,
Always leavin' my heart on the line for the
worst of men,
But this time, the golden ticket's mine.

He Has A Way

Of taking me from a life
where breathing was hard
and
crying was easy.
Whether we're miles apart.
or
My hand rests closely upon his heart,
He helps me forget all the things
I'll never miss.
 All I feel is
his tender kiss.
All I see are
his eyes gazing at me.
All I hear are
his sweet words in my ear.

Homesick

Not aiming for some pie in the sky
Not for a dream come true
Not wishing on a shining star
The only thing I am waiting on is you,
And wondering where you are.

Not looking to get rich,
Not needing some grand, far-off adventure
Not searching for a perfect place to lay my head—
The only thing I am waiting on is you,
And wondering where you are.

All those things are nice and all,
But they're not what I need.
I need a man who simply sees the need
To be with me.

I've looked for so long,
But no matter how hard I try,
I'm homesick for the man
Who's homesick for me—
Who knows that feeling,
But until now, couldn't see
What he was homesick and looking for
Was, simply,
Me.

How Long Is a Life?

How long is a life, anyway?
Not that moment when we take our final
breath,
but the moment you look back
And realize you've had your
last intimate moment with a lover.
When your children head out on their own
and home will forever have a void of life.
Or the end of life as you knew it,
as you stop breathing for an instant as a
parent stops breathing forever,
leaving you an orphan.
Perhaps, when you walk through your empty
house left alone
and you reach over in the darkness to the
empty side of the bed
knowing it will forever remain untouched.
So how long is a life?
It is a long passage, a journey
filled, at first, with happiness
giving way to many deaths.

I Believe In. . .

I believe in. . .
Glances that tell each other things no one else
can hear
Laughs shared over silly things making up the
important things and knowing we are getting
this right
The easy fit of our lives after being apart
The melding from you and me and how easy
it becomes we

I believe in. . .
The man that you are
Your gentleness
Your honesty
The way you love me so tenderly.

I believe in. . .
Trust, as you have taught me
Like I have never known before

Becoming a Mom

The moment that small creature is placed in your
arms,
The moment they take their first breath, the
breath is knocked out of your lungs—
That moment when you realize this tiny person is
going to share their life with you,
And you get to watch, you realize, in that split
second, that you are the one
That those tiny eyes will look to for
(let's be honest)
The next thirty years for guidance.
And you need to know the answers.
You hold on so tight in that moment,
and they hold on so tight in that moment
and even though they don't know it,
You do.
This is the beginning of something magical
Something life altering.
Yes, when you found you were expecting, it was
life altering, but right now in this moment,
this tiny person looks to you; their life in your
hands,
Waiting on you to work magic
And you will-
You are now a mom.
And you will.

boy's club

she grew up listening to their chords
watching them make love with their strings
without even realizing it, she fell hard not for the
guys,
but the fire in her soul their rhythm would bring.

her little girl self, at her daddy's knee,
sat mesmerized by the twang and the tap of his
toes
but it was their boy's club—
they never handed her the key

it was nothing new,
this love of the strings the family always knew
why couldn't they see
that she, too, fell in love with the strings

it was news to all—especially to her
but really she was sure—she never needed what
another love could bring
she realized she can make love to her own 6 string
when stroked by her own hands

Daddy

Daddy

Fireflies shine in my night sky
Safe there thanks to Daddy's tender humanity
Piano keys dance as Daddy's fingers once slid
across the board
The strings on his guitar sing
Just as if his fingers still lent sound to the
frets
Harmony mingles now from my lips, placed
there by Daddy's enduring love
Tears shed of sadness drift into those of joy
His touch felt on my cheek as surely as if his
own hand still touched my face

In a Moment

I lived and died in a moment
Sighed as I realized it was over
Watched you walk away
When I told you good-bye today

But, the sun will keep shining
I'll keep running toward the next day
Nothing's ever kept me down long
I'm too damn strong for that

Making Love to the Guitar

My love's first love is his guitar
Yes, he's quiet and strong
and plays me like a song
That moves my feet and melts my heart

I am not my love's first love
I've always known that from the start
My love's first love is his guitar
I see it written across his face
I feel it echo in my heart
He makes love with the strings
But he kisses my soul with the sound that he
brings

On stage, I know I lose the man to the music
So gently, at times, he lifts the guitar to his
chest
Caressing the frets like he caresses my hair
Right now, he's lost in his song as I stare
longingly
Knowing the quiet of the night will allow him
To surrender his mind and soul to me

Our First Dance

The night is long and dark, and you're so far away
It feels like forever since I touched your face
How could something be deeply rooted in such a
short span of time
It seems within moments, your sweet spirit
soaked into my soul
Urging my pen to paper to capture some
semblance of rhyme

In seconds my body melted into yours on the
dance floor
For all that I was not looking for, you were oh so
much more
You took not just my hand that night, but
somehow my heart, and it just knew
It was always you! My search was through!

Don't let me awaken to find you were just a dream
For though it seems like a fairytale, that is not
what I need
Just you and me, simply together, for what's left
of this ride called
Life.

Painted on Smile

My wounds have healed
Sealed with the truth
You hadn't moved on
But you were gone
From the beginning

Words of love slipped
From your lips building me up
To break me down
Yet, months passed since last
You crossed my mind

And here I am ripping open the scar
Even though you are so far away
Little by little, the miles grew longer
The hurt grew stronger
I sealed up the truth—that I had crafted this hell
I alone allowed myself to fall

Now, I pretend to be happy in life
With the direction I'm taking
I paint on a smile as I head out the door
So no one can see
The real me. But at night, when I
close the door tight and turn out the light
my heart breaks for I can't bear the ache anymore

Where the Crest Falls Away

Why is it that I must leave
to find my way home?
I must lose myself to the darkness
to find my way to the light.

I must always fight
to escape the horrors of endless nights,
The torments of my soul
for some semblance of feeling whole.

Finding solace in the rolling tide
somewhere-out there- my heart drifts,
tossed, lost at sea,
until I landed on this rocky beach.

The sea's salty spray
gently, unceasingly reminds me
there's peace somewhere out there,
Where the crest quietly slips away.

The List

Ladies, did you know
there are lists floating about
waiting to snatch you up?
be careful where you tread
where you lay your head
bed with the wrong player,
and you may find your name
in red on the Devil's List

Many of us
-risk takers at heart-
may enjoy the part of vixen
...for awhile,
but, in the end, it's the reputation
that suffers the most collateral damage,
when dirty hands stain your name
and mistake you as one and the same.

Ladies of Substance

Small towns, so often built by the Haves
On the backs of the Have-Nots
In these often tiny, toxic havens
reside a small, pathetic group
of Haves wives, and Haves exes,
who fail to see they'll never be,
in their contrived society,
true Ladies of Substance.

Making their appearances,
the label on their clothes,
the street on which they live—
will never give them what they need
to succeed in making that stellar list
for they missed, when they were born,
the only key to becoming, one day,
a Lady of Substance.

For Class is an innate style,
where pretenders shine for mere moments
but class within Ladies of Substance
shines for a lifetime.

Share Cropper's Lover

Cold hands found her spine in the dark
His presence sensed before his touch
The stark reality held the truth of power,
Holding her in place without a ring, a name, or
money
She, his pawn, he played the board—
Within all the circles, his name soared above the
others.
He bothered not to conceal his indiscretions,
Left splayed across the lips of all the knights, the
kings, the queens.
She was seen and yet invisible,
Two sides of the field, he maintained:
Hers dust-littered fields with illiterates
unnamed-unclaimed
The other pristine- unstained.

Decades passed- bigotry cast
A heritage, a background once served.
Once ironically shamed; now with honor claimed.
In the end, a wee little thing
From an honourable outcast
Would put right the honor in his name,
Erase the pretentious shame.

A Darkened Woods

The little things
- they say-
that are supposed to bring two hearts
together
Are not really enough to help you weather it
out
the passion shared for what you both cared
most about
weaving what you believed to be knots of love
within your hearts
were threads easily snipped, slipped through
your fingers.

Scenes viewed through a microscope
reveal shared passions, quiet moments, and
stolen kisses—
now, missed chances at what could've been.
music once shared, the Steel,
in the heart has become part of the memories
in a darkened Woods.

Safe

Safe is elusive
The heart once rested within arms,
wrapped tightly no fear- no thought of loss.
but loss came like a thief in the night,
and stole that safety away.
Since that day, the heart, the head, and the
soul have been
in constant turmoil.
Peace will never come again.
Safe is elusive
A long-lost friend.

Winter Lake

Winter's chill settling
in the early morning lake,
mingles with its inner warmth
gray-tinged mist softly drifts
towards pink skies,
just before the sun fully awakens—
mirrored on the water's gentle crests,
winding their way to shore,
the only sound in the broken silence.

Glimpses of Time

Where did the time go?
Yesterday, I held you both in my arms,
cuddled you close,
Protected you from harm.
I blink, and see
you playing, laughing—
I kiss your scraped knees
It seems as if the very next day
You both found your wings,
And you flew away.
But I stayed so you would
Know your way.
But now, my heart is warmed
as I see you seek out safety
in another's arms
offering calm through your storms.

Finally

The words were spoken
That should have been
uttered so long ago
Pain ebbs and flows away
Still, you carry me
Along like the tide-gently
Hiding your true feelings
So I won't see that
Even though we looked
So perfect for each other
You were never going
To leave another.

Alone

Alone
Was a choice I made
Even before it was thrust upon me.
As strong as I am,
Sometimes the walls come crashing in,
Hurling me back to the weakened me
I used to be.
Alone,
Offers me a chance to breathe,
To mend a heart and soul once broken and lost
In years of words that cut to the bone—
And marks not left behind on the body,
forever etched like carvings of stone in the mind
Alone,
I take a breath and step off that ledge.
For a moment, I will feel sorry for myself,
But I am stronger than this.
Only I can reclaim my strength.
Alone,
Is a choice I made,
Even before it was thrust upon me.
But I refuse to let the walls cave in
I'm fiercer than I've ever been.
Alone
Is my choice
I'll make it every day
Unless I decide to choose another way.

As the Rain Poured

Cuts on my feet bleed deeper than before
With every broken shard that drops from my
heart to the floor
but, baby, you weren't meant for me- I see that
now
Really, I knew it from that first night, as the rain
poured but you showed up at my door
We started on this path, your hand on my thigh as
we talked quietly in the dark that night
With that first kiss in the soft green lights as you
said good-bye
We tiptoed around it
Pretended nothing was there,
Upended all that we knew to be right but every
stare was electric—
A magnet between you and me
Stolen afternoons between the sheets were stolen
from the one you have at home
Do you think she really didn't know you were
cheating every time you were leaving?
She didn't know where you were going?
Now, this is gonna hurt. I am the one left grieving
a love that wasn't even mine.

Where My Heart Dwells

It starts with the drive through the country dotted with black faced sheep. Tension begins to lift, and a feeling of joy starts to slowly seep into my very marrow. When I make that last right turn off the narrow road, I know I am on my descent to the sea and my little cottage- where my heart dwells.

When the village comes into view below me, the North Sea's cascades to my left, I stop and take it in-drink it in- like mother's milk. The waves lap along the pebble shore and over the old fishing pier, if I make it there at high tide. The village sits silently awaiting my arrival. Patiently, I begin my slow, precarious drive down the tiny path. Holding my breath, I make the hairpin turn halfway down in my little European rental being careful not to kill the engine on the manual transmission. It takes skill that I do not have so nerves are kept in check only by my ironclad determination that I can do this! It isn't like I haven't done it before.

The tiny parking lot, next to the sea wall now on my right, is at the bottom with its cottage storage buildings on my left. Wheelbarrows prop up against each one acting as valets for residents with more "stuff" than hands can carry.

Scottish weather is almost always cloudy and wet, and the biting cold off of the water almost always gives me a "chilly" reception but this has never been a deterrent. Even sunny days are deceptive to the novice visitor. My bag holds all I need to welcome the outdoors as my cottage welcomes me. My wellies, my raincoat, and my numerous socks, gloves, mittens, and scarves (even in the middle of summer) serves as armor to enjoy this little niche in the world where my heart dwells, and it awaits my arrival as I unpack the car. My soul is here! I anxiously get a death grip on my belongings to make my short trek along the shell and stone path to my little #10 yellow and blue cottage.

My feet automatically propel me past time-and weather-worn cottages and up the hill. I turn the key to the little latched blue door, and it softly creaks open. My heart smiles. I'm home!

I put my case in the bedroom and climb the witch stairs to the kitchen and living room and say, "Hello" to my heart that waits to welcome me back. My fingers already itch to start a fire in the little wood stove and turn on the blue Turkish lamp chandelier hanging from the vaulted living room ceiling. Its beauty has become so soothing to me that I leave it on throughout my visit and now have them in the same soothing blue hues in my own living room in the states. My routine is always to pour myself a whisky and settle myself on the sofa watching the day retire over the sea while I enjoy an evening of soft music, a crackling fire, and writing.

Tomorrow, perhaps, I will don my wellies and walk the beach looking for perfect pebbles and make my way around the cliffs to Gardenstown for scones and a cuppa at the little tea shop and pick up some other provisions at the store, but for now. . . well. . . for now, my heart and I are happy in our cottage by the sea in Crovie.

Phoenix

Sunlight dances across my face
My eyelashes flutter as I pause
To catch the warmth.
In the moment, that slightest breath of time,
The knowledge of how I've grown
Flickers gently through my mind,
Reminding me I've found my way.

My heart is in one piece,
My soul has learned how to embrace the darkness.
Somehow, I've learned to walk a little taller,
And laugh a little louder,
And a little more. . .

It no longer matters what has passed
Out of pain came Me.
They say a phoenix rises out of the ashes
I'm dusting them off my shoulders
And flying higher than I ever thought I could.

My thoughts, my dreams are on my loved ones
Still here, who only want what's best for me.
Now I can help them soar—
I need not the old me anymore.
My ashes drift away.